Something

To Think About

>>> >>>

By
Netheldia Sheree Porter

Something to think about!

Exceptional children are special to God and they have special purposes and missions set aside for their lives. This is why we cannot use alcohol and drugs because they keep us bound and keeps us from hearing from God. This in turn makes it impossible for us to accomplish the mission and carry out the plans that he has for our lives. "Learning daily from life's experiences and growing from past mistakes, each morning I arise longing to be a better person than I was yesterday".

Netheldia S. Porter

Table of Content

Chapter 1

What's wrong with me

In the beginning we sometimes have a hard time accepting that we are powerless and our lives had become unmanageable because the sense of powerlessness may represent a sign of weakness in "well put together individuals". It may force an individual who has had the freedom to make choices over the events in their lives to come to the realization that something is wrong and they cannot fix it.

Nonetheless, despite this recognition, we are not totally ignorant to the fact that things will go wrong at one point or another in our lives. Generally speaking, we have a natural instinct to want to fix the problem, but often times we fail to administer the right solutions to

address the situation. I would say that this comes from the lack of knowledge and/or the inability to deal with painful issues effectively.

Surprisingly I have found that if an issue is not dealt with at the root "like a weed" it keeps coming back to haunt us and causes malfunctions, distraction, and trouble in our lives.

Tell yourselves "we must get to the root of the problem". Therefore once an individual comes to the conclusion that no matter what they do or try, the problem still exists, they are now ready to admit that they are powerless over the situation, and come to terms with the fact that the problem is bigger than them. Acknowledging that we cannot fix it alone does not have to be a bad experience simply because we are human and we just cannot fix everything ourselves or better yet, we all need help sometimes. It's okay, it's a part of life, and I am here to share with you some important principles to not only live a successful life, but to help you relax, enjoy and accept life for what it really is—beautiful and worth living.

Many people who are addicts feel like they do not have a problem. We tell ourselves "I don't drink or use that much" or "I can control my alcohol and/or drug intake, or I only do it on weekends or after work". Sadly this is far from the truth because we cannot control our intake. Believe it or not, each and every last one of us started out with "simple using" which over time got out of control.

Basically I believe that it is important for an individual to learn all they can about why their bodies react like it does to alcohol and drugs, and why we are powerless over our addiction, and why we can never use again. I am not a doctor, but I will share with you information that I learned during my studies on addictive behaviors. "The way I understood it".

Alcohol and drugs have chemicals in them that affect the cells in the human brain and other organs. These generic (man made chemicals) take over the natural chemicals that our brain and body use to reproduce cells which helps our body function properly, smoothly and effectively. The human body is amazing because we have little micro cells that can only be seen through a special microscope that are always reproducing themselves. This is what keeps us alive!

Nevertheless, when we drink alcohol or use drugs, we throw off this natural function, and our brain and organs starts to rely on the poison chemicals to reproduce the cells instead-- which causes the alcohol or drugs over time to keep us functioning. It's almost like putting the wrong kind of oil, transmission fluid or gas in your car "it will only go so far before it breaks down". Our bodies does not break down this fast, but by doing drugs and drinking alcohol, it's a work in progress!

Moreover once we stop putting drugs and alcohol in our system, our bodies begin to crave these chemicals. Sometimes it is very painful causing what is known as "withdrawals'. Often times it is these pains and craving that keep us wanting more alcohol and drugs which causes us to give our bodies what we think it wants or better yet, what we think it needs. Gracefully after a prolonged time of not using, our normal cell chemicals and other organ functions returns, and react as usual or "normal".

Boastfully speaking, I am thankful for those times when I slept for two or three days in a row because it gave my body time to repair itself. Remember anything that causes your body not to function properly is a sickness or illness therefore alcohol and drug addiction is a disease.

Have you ever been around a group of people and notice that some of them can drink and stop for a long period of time? Or they do not even get "sloppy drunk", or they say that they had enough. These people are called moderate or social drinkers, and they do not have this imbalance in their brain. But we as alcoholics and drug addicts do, and the very minute that we put these poisonous chemicals back into our bodies, the brain goes "Oh yeah!-now I remember" and begins to feed off of the alcohol and drugs once again. We can never drink or use drugs because our brains and bodies will have the same reaction each and every single time—even after years of not drinking or using.

NEVER means NEVER! I do not care how you try to switch or limit the use, it may always affect you the same way. Therefore my friends, we are powerless over our addiction because we will never be able to control the way our bodies chemically react to the substances.

Some of us tried to control our drinking and drug use, but our bodies just kept wanting more and more over long periods of time. Basically we develop a relationship with what we are addicted to. Even more so, if anybody tried to tell us we had a problem, we would deny it and come up with all sorts of explanations, and rationalizations for our uses. Sadly over time we not only lose control of our addiction, but our daily lives starts to deteriorate, as we began to vacate reality, and make our beds in the false reality that we created, and expect everyone else around us to survive in. (We will talk more about this later).

After prolonged misuse of anything, we began to have problems in our relationships, at work or school, with other family members, and within our community. Furthermore, we lose all sense of reality and began to neglect our obligations to ourselves, as well as our families. For instance, the rent and bills stop getting paid, we stop eating properly, and we even neglect our children and our health.

To sum it up, our lives became unmanageable. We began to tell ourselves, our spouses, employers, teachers, or any other person that may be generally concerned that we do not have a problem. Let me tell you all this, you cannot fix what you will not admit is broken! Self-denial is public enemy number one for any type of addiction. Until we can come to terms with our addiction, we will continue to suffer from this conning disease.

Despite the chemical imbalance, the root reasons that we may drink or use drugs, or have any other type of abusive behavior in the first place needs to be addressed. Many of the problems and behavior started back in our childhood. I will say that it is very important that you start opening up to your counselor, sponsor, or another person that you trust about those issues.

One final thing, we are not just powerless over alcohol and drugs, but I want you to keep in mind that we are powerless over people, places, and things. I will touch a little on these things later. At any rate, do not be hard on yourself. I understand that it is painful and hard for some people to admit that they are powerless or that they have mismanaged their lives.

Something to think about!

Psalm 69:1-3 Save me, O God! For the waters have come up to my neck. I sink in deep mire. Where there is no standing; I have come into deep waters, where the floods overflow me. I am weary with my crying; My throat is dry; My eyes fail while I wait for my God. Guess what? Whatever your prayer may be or has been, he heard you, and he does answer prayers.

Welcome to the first day of the rest of your life!

Chapter 2

Power

Before I go any further, give yourselves a hand for still being here—making it through another day "one day at a time".
Furthermore, for those of you who feel unsure about reading this book, you are in the right place, at the right time. You know what? There are a lot of people who want to help, but do not know how to get it, or do not believe that it is possible to recover. You have to be sick and tired of being sick and tired. Which brings me to the fact that we must believe in the power to restore us back to sanity and make us whole. Believe it or not, this is the same power that guided you here!

Can you think of a situation that you couldn't see your way out of and for some strange reason you felt that you should have been dead, in jail, lights cut off, fired from your job, or homeless? Well it's like this. That same higher power that helped you get through those terrible, and what may have looked like endless and hopeless situations, is the same power that can also help restore you to sanity and make you whole. It is that same power that helps you get and stay clean and sober, loving and caring about yourself and the life that you live, as well as another human being.

What is sanity? Well it means soundness of mind, mentally stable, and having soundness of judgment. Think about that "soundness of judgment", I do not know about you, but when I was in my addiction my judgment was way off!! Especially when I thought that I could control my drug and alcohol intake and use. We as addicts lose all sanity during our substance abuse. We thought that we could hide it, go to work with it, have a normal relationship while using it, control it, and so much more.

What is insane? To keep doing the same things over and over again expecting a different result . This is important for well put together people to remember (you do not have to be pronounced clinically crazy to be insane). That's what we did! I call this self-inflicted pain. You know when we got loaded-- we acted crazy and deranged! The things we did were-impractical! The way we lived our lives where very foolish! But GOD "a higher power" can restore us back to soundness and cause us to be mentally stable.

What is wholeness? It means to be complete, uninjured, functioning, undivided, and being as one with society. I know that many of us through our drinking and substance abuse fell short and lost a lot of things. For some of us even our health is/was affected. Alcohol and drug abuse destroys many of our bodies' natural function. For example: our lives, brain, estrogen, stomach, bloodstream, heart, and more. Using substances and drinking may cause strokes, heart attacks, high blood pressure, digestion problem and more. (By the way smoking cigarettes causes a lot of health problems as well) .

PEOPLE! We cannot function as a whole if we are addicted to anything !! Our minds have a genetic disorder, this means that our brain reacts differently than a normal or moderate drinker. I do not care how you alter the drug, or how you change the type of alcohol you drink, or try to control the intake or amount. It will never work. Sorry! The chemicals in our brains do not function right when altered them with these poisonous chemicals (alcohol and drugs). We were built like this. Furthermore, I do believe that we were created special for a special purpose by our higher power. Therefore when we put these chemicals in our bodies, we get way off the mark of the purpose for our lives. This statement right here is another lesson for another day. When we talk about being restored to wholeness it speaks on many levels. For example keeping a job, family, intimate relationships, and being healthy mentally, emotionally, physically, and spiritually.

Gracefully speaking a power higher than ourselves can restore all these things back to us. For those who never knew how to function in these areas, a higher power can introduce these things to you because you need these things to live life effectively. We tried to fix all these things ourselves, and 9 times out of 10 we only made the situation worse (this is the insanity part). So with the realization of a power greater than ourselves, we began to take positive steps within our sobriety. We have already realized that we are powerless and our life is unmanageable. Let me say this. We are human, and we ALL make mistakes, we mess up. Last I heard no one was perfect but Jesus Christ. Life goes on! Your life goes on. Pinch yourselves. See you are not dead, therefore your life can be fixed, "one day at a time" and a power greater than yourself can help you accomplish this.

SOMETHING TO THINK ABOUT!

Do you know that alcohol, and cigarettes are the most deadliest drugs on the market and they cause more health problems and deaths than any other drug? Have you noticed that they both are legal!! Ask yourself WHY? Have you noticed that alcohol is cheaper in the lower class neighborhoods, and are sold on just about every other street corner? Have you noticed that upper class people drive down to ghetto neighborhoods to purchase most of their drugs? People this system is setup to keep you handcuffed, incarcerated and bound to the disease of alcoholism and drug abuse, all to keep you stuck! It's a trap, and we do not even see it. Sadly, the only ones that are keeping us trap is ourselves. You have to take a stand and fight for your life and the lives of your children, loved ones and communities. This is not going to stop.

Think about what is happening to our society, our children and our livelihood.

Netheldia S. Porter

Chapter 3

Decision Time

Now I want you to tell yourself "I have to make a decision, and it has got to be between me and my higher power". We as addicts have spent most of our lives living for ourselves. We have allowed alcohol and drugs to become our commander and chief. We have spent so much time doing things the way we wanted to do them, to where we have gotten so deep into being our own gods, " we gotten off and far from the plans that our higher power has for our lives". Therefore as stated earlier, our lives have become unmanageable and we need help from a higher power--I chose to call mines God, Jehovah, I am that I am-- "LET GO AND LET GOD".

When you turn your life, your will and your way over to your higher power, you are doing what I call "surrendering". Once you make this decision you are basically saying "God I cannot do this, I give it all to you, my will and my life, let your will be done". Let me say the more you pray and talk to God, the more you will begin to trust this power. In addition, the more sober you are, the more you will be able to hear this power guiding you to the plans for your life. Remember when we were high and loaded we heard what we wanted to hear, we walked and talked about how we wanted to, and we lived according to what we felt was best for our lives. We made a mess out of it — didn't we!

Do you all know that your higher power has a plan for each and every last one of you? Are you all aware that this plan for your life is different from anyone else? You

have to be willing to trust your
higher power, and know that you
will be guided in the right direction,
and you will not be lead wrong! For
some of us, we will be kicking and
screaming because during the course
of this transition you will find
yourself fighting yourself. This
happens because we are used to
being our own boss, and pride will
get in the way. Some people struggle
because of their own self-will
"control freaks". To some it will feel
like having the ground underneath
us removed, and you will fight to
gain balance and security. For some
of us if we cannot feel ourselves
working things out in our own lives
we feel lost and weak. Once again
"let go and let God have control.

Making the decision to turn your
will and life over to the care of your
higher power will be one of the most
major advances you will make
during your recovery and spiritual

growth. Let me say this and mark my words, YOU CAN NOT DO THIS WITHOUT SURRENDERING. Yeah it may last for a few days or months, but trust me you will only take one more trip around the same old mountain! When you give up the ghost, you will have more peace and less stress. Stuff that used to bother you will not bother you or not as much anymore. Believe me you will get a sense of contentment beyond definition.

Let's do this together: (1) Close your eyes. (2) Quiet your mind and put to silence every thought. (3) Breath in and out slowly. (4) Allow yourself to drift in pure silence. (5) Feel yourself standing before God "like you are standing before a King". (6) Bow yourself to that authority and allow your inner-child to come out "he said come before me as little children". (7) Imagine yourself kneeling before the throne . (8) Begin to feel the peace and presence of God. (9) Talk to God. (10) LISTEN to all honesty and then obey.

One of the greatest things about surrendering to God is that YOU DO NOT HAVE TO BE PERFECT. Just go as you are. Will you make mistakes sometimes, YES!! But when you fall GET-UP!

Chapter 4

The Look Within

Repeat after me "I need to do some soul searching and acknowledge somethings about me-me-me". The finger is pointing in the mirror, but the thumb is pointing back at YOU!

Let me first say that this does not have anything to do with the past, but everything to do with who you are right now. Soul searching allows us to check out the positive and the negative things about ourselves, as we are today, as well as identifying our strengths and limitations—and accepting them. Yes thee magic word "excepting" --owning up. Believe me you will become a better person to yourself and the world around you when you accept yourself for who you are--the good, the bad, and the ugly!

Basically, the more we come to terms with the person we are today, the easier it is for us to see and put childish and negative behavior behind us. I read where a man said, "When I was a child, I thought as a child, I acted like a child. Now I am a grown man--it's time to put childish things behind me". Searching ourselves, helps us put hurtful childish behavior and memories behind us, and grow more into maturity, with the help of God. Soul searching helps us to get to the root of our behaviors, and causes us to be honest with ourselves about ourselves by reexamining our personalities, strengths, and limitations.

Another word is self-realization. Some people (addicts or not) do inventory on themselves once in a while for positive changes in their lives. Therefore, it's okay to check yourself out once in a while. Believe me the older we get some of "our ways" are just not becoming! Therefore it's time to move on to the next phase of life. Moreover, we should know not only acknowledge the things we can and cannot do, but we must be able to accept these limitations.

We all have physical, mental, and/or emotional limitations. One good way to do a self-inventory is to fold a piece of paper in half and on one side write your strengths and on the other side write your weaknesses or limitations. For example one's strength could be leadership, responsible, trustworthy, or being reliable: One's weakness could be lazy, procrastinator, unreliable, or lack of integrity, just to name a few.

Nonetheless, when you do this pray about both of them, and be honest because you are not a surprise to God. Remember this-- if you lie, you will not be lying to no one but yourself. You are here to make a change in your life, so keep it real! You only hurt yourself when you lie to yourself about YOU! While you are doing this also acknowledge resentments and fears — and talk about them with God, counselor or another human being that you trust. To add please do not get into an argument with the people around you because this is about you. If you feel yourself getting moody or resentful get to yourself because sometimes dealing with our resentments or fears causes us to become angry. Just know that this is a personal growth exercise and it is to help you with your rehabilitation process.

Something to think about!

"BE THEE TRUE TO THY OWN SELF" *Do you know who you are? Do you know where you are in life? Are you 40 years old and still acting like you are 20? You know it is a saying that whatever age you started using and abusing alcohol and drugs, that's the age you stop growing. If you don't figure out who you are, your past and people around you will define and determine who you are! "Oh he is just a crack, speed or meth head; yeah! she's just a lying abusive alcoholic; oh he's just a thief, and a cheater; she's just a big dummy, he's retarded, he ain't never been nothing and never will be nothing". Don't be named by your past situations, behaviors or experiences. Ask God to show you – yourself!*

Netheldia S. Porter

Chapter 5

I Apologize

Next, open your mouth and confess!! Yes, it is time to look at your past. Remember as I told you before, you are not a surprise to God he already knows all about you! Therefore while confessing remember God is a loving, merciful, gracious, and a forgiving God, and loves you unconditionally. You can hide and lie to yourself and other people about your past, but you cannot lie to God. Also know this, what goes on in the dark ALWAYS comes to the light.

Now before you began, pray and ask your higher power to support you, and give you strength, while you confess. Confessing and admitting your wrongs is mainly and purely being true to yourself. It's facing up and owning up to the wrong YOU did.

Remember you cannot fix what you won't admit is broken! It's something like exposing the innermost you. I tell you this, if you can face up to the truth about the wrongs you have done and talk to yourself and your higher power first, then someone else, you will have taken another big and major step in your rehabilitation process. Nevertheless, let me warn you of this, "YOU HAVE TO BE CAREFUL WHO YOU SHARE YOUR WRONGS WITH" because some people will hold them against you! It is better to tell a pastor, your sponsor, your counselor or someone you truly trust—again trust, and a safely disclose your secrets to.

Many of you may be asking, why you should tell anyone at all? Well when you confess things out of your mouth you are openly letting your higher power, yourself and another person know that you acknowledge the wrong. It is something about confession and hearing the words out loud coming out of your own mouth that frees the soul. It really feels like a burden lifted up off of you. We walk around with so much guilt and shame on us, don't you think it is a good idea to be freed of some of it? It's a part of healing! You cannot heal a wound that remains open! So get it up off of you. Now some of the wrong things that some of us have done may incriminate us. I understand and in situations like this, just tell your higher power and ask for forgiveness. Nonetheless, no matter what your situation is, forgive YOURSELF as well! Let that baggage go! Life is too short and is moving on--move on with it--WHOLE heading towards the mark of SANITY! Remember that none of us are perfect "we all fall short of the glory".

Now when we start talking to people about our wrongs, we must also be willing to listen with an open mind to any suggestions. It is okay for the individual you share with to give their input. Remember you have been wrong for a long time and your ways have not been working--remember the definition of insanity? This is a good step toward wholeness. So let them speak! You might learn something, it just might help you not to repeat destructive behaviors.

Now some of us are a little more rebellious than others and some old behaviors are hard to break. But get it off of YOU, and let your higher power do the job of fixing you--remember, you are not your own god or no one else's for that matter. Your God may not come

when you want, but your God will
be RIGHT on time. You did not get
in this situation overnight, and it's
not going to change over night. You
have to be fully committed for the
long haul in the process of your
recovery! Remember your higher
power grace is enough. In other
words, you are covered--despite it
ALL sweetheart! We grow from
glory to glory. Not in your
neighbors timing or your partners,
or kids, but in your higher power's
glory and timing, as your personal
relationship grows with him. That's
why you turned your life over to
your higher power as you
understand and grow in the new or
renewed relationship.

Nonetheless, you have to open
your mouth and admit you're
wrong--saying it out loud! It does
not make you less than a person to
say "I was wrong or I made a
mistake, and this is what I-I-I did".

Watch out for "PRIDE" it will get you caught up and keep you in trouble, bonded, set back and unchanged--EVERY time! Let the words flow out of your mouth, unrehearsed in your mind. It will be an inner peace beyond explanation or understanding!

Once you ask your higher power to forgive you. IT'S FORGIVEN AND FORGOTTEN. If you misbehave again--confess again! State the wrong, and move on! Trust me with sincere work, the behavior will change over time.

Whatever you do, don't give up on God because even when it seems like it, God has not given up on you. Just keep seeking and asking for help. Truthfully, your God knew what you were going to do before you did it!

Something to think about!

"Confession is good for the spirit, refreshes the heart, bring peace to the mind, and frees the soul"

Netheldia S. Porter

Chapter 6

Change !

Repeat after me "I'm sick and tired of being sick and tired-- God please remove my ineffective behavior". Okay, now first I want you to be careful about asking your higher power for what you want over what you need. In other words when talking to God be careful about saying "I want to be this or that; or I want this to happen or that" because at this point you are in God's business, and being demanding. Remember as I stated earlier "you are turning over your will and your ways". Therefore ask like this "I need help with this or that", or even, "your will be done in my life not mines" It allows your God to do what's best-- guide you in the way you should go. It's acknowledging the fact that you are aware of your problems or situations, and you do not know how to fix them or how to orchestrate your life. This goes back to surrendering!

Now at this point we are totally ready to open the door between us and God, and to have a more personal relationship with him. It also lets God know that you trust him, and you are really ready to work with him and not again him. As you follow through "wholeheartedly" with your rehabilitation process, you will change. Some of you have already changed in ways you haven't even noticed However, other people around you may have noticed--for instance, since you started reading this book! Nonetheless I bet, if you look hard enough, you could see some behavior or ways you use to have, or ways you use to think, that you no longer have or do. At any rate keep reading this book and before you know it you'll be telling yourself it's been a long time since I thought about this or that, or even done this or that. My friends this is an example of the power of your higher power working in your life!

We have already admitted that we are powerless over people, places, things, drugs and alcohol. We know that without our higher power, we can do nothing. Most of us have surrendered, confessed, and asked for forgiveness.

Now it's time to build an even stronger relationship with your God. Through this process the bad will begin to leave, and the good-- that's already in us, will start to reveal itself even more. Frankly, it has always been there, but it was not given a fair chance to reveal itself effectively. Mainly because some just got used to the way we were right or wrong . Some of us were inappropriately taught the difference between right and wrong so, it's not our fault. Then sadly, some of us, just plain old did not care.

But when we partner with our God, he slowly begins to show us what's right--and once you learn right, you can't unlearn it! Society itself with all its changes and demands can put challenges on one's life, as well as one's beliefs. So every once in a while it is good to ask him to also renew our hearts and minds and remove anything that is not of him from us. Trust me, a lot of stuff may start coming to your attention as wrong or untrue that you once believed or thought was right! Once again some will change and grow move faster than others, but no matter what the pace is, do not give up on God.

Now, you might continue to keep some ineffective behaviors. But know that God is looking at your heart-- day in and day out--because he who has begun a good work in you shall not fail, and he is not through with you yet. It will happen! You just keep on loving and building a solid relationship with him. For those of you who do not know what ineffective behaviors are--in this matter. They are past behaviors once starting the recovery process that set you back. It's also character flaws like impatient, anger, bitterness, jealousy, manipulations and lying just to name a few. We all have character flaws, and when you partner with God, he will help you acknowledge, and work through them.

Sorry, but yes! Some of us are going to need a little more help than others. But when you work in partnership with God and not

against him, you will be more
effective.

Something to think about!

Underneath all of that pain you feel, the trouble and trauma you've caused, your confusion, disappointments, and uncertainty. There is a wonderful, strong, powerful, confident, radiant, able to withstand anything child of God! You are the apple of God's eye, and he got your back. Don't let anybody tell you differently.

Netheldia S.Porter

Chapter 7

Humble Yourself

You are doing fine. You have read a lot. Do not stop now. Keep up the good work!! Knowledge enhances and enables life!

Humbleness is the root of our recovery. Therefore humbly ask God to remove your shortcomings and downfalls. Truthfully speaking, the more we humble ourselves the more we will have the desire to seek God in our life's. The closer we get to this power, the more humble we become. I will tell you something that I have learned, without some kind of relationship with God, it's almost impossible to stay clean and sober. This is why earlier we partner with our higher power. So now by asking him to remove our shortcomings, the partnership will go hand in hand.

Now we cannot expect God to do all of the work, we have to do our part. Therefore, if we truthfully and honestly did some soul searching, and took that inventory of ourselves, we should have brought to light many of our shortcomings and downfalls. Furthermore, the more we free ourselves of these character defects, the more peace, serenity, happiness and manageability we will have in our lives (as a reminder--we have already discovered that we are powerless and our lives have become unmanageable). Say out loud with me, "God grant me the serenity to accept the things I cannot change, the courage to change the things I can and the wisdom to know the difference". Now take a deep breath!

Unfortunately, everything we ask to be removed may not go away all at one time. Remember, one of the major keys to your sobriety besides partnering with God, is to take it "one day at a time". Truthfully, if God gave us everything at one time, we wouldn't be able to handle it!

My friends, we grow into maturity and that doesn't happen overnight, and for sure age has nothing to do with it. That's why you can be 60 years old and still learning things about yourself and life. Our God will not put more on us then we can bear. Believe me, what someone else can bear, you might not be able to, and vice versa. Be patient while you are waiting on God, and just know that "he is not through with you yet"!

You know it's a good feeling at the end of the day knowing that you put your best foot forward and as I say, "nothing beats a failure but a try". Nonetheless, some days will be alright, and some days will not, and someday you just are not going to feel like trying at all. It happens because we are not perfect. But, I assure you, the closer you get to God, the more you will be able to feel when you are slipping--talk to him about it. Some of you may ask for how long? I believe for as long as it takes for you to overcome and process your victory. So don't beat yourself up, and learn to forgive yourself, as God forgives you. A prayer of mine that I pray is "God help me to be a better person today then I was yesterday". This doesn't means that you were a bad person yesterday, but it signals to God that you want to go higher in certain areas of your life. It is important to remember-- you are not a surprise to God.

Our inner-child was damaged and caused us to not mature right as adults. We have to love that child through a new growth, ourselves "with the help of God" into a healthy spiritual, mental, and emotional adult being. Therefore sweetheart, anyway that you may see yourself growing, give God and yourself some praise. Most of all, give thanks to him because we grow from glory to glory--remember, in his timing. What God does for you, he will do it right, and it will last forever--he makes no mistakes. Remember, no one can stop you from growing and changing but you! All of us have an area of immaturity, and our pride stops us from admitting this. I am going to tell you the truth about something. We will always have things and ways that we will need to change. It's called life and growing old. It happens! Come to terms with it!

Now we will never eliminate all of our negative thoughts or behaviors because once again we are NOT PERFECT; and if anyone feels like they are the "perfect child of

God" they are just lying to themselves. Even religious and spiritual leaders make mistakes. Being clean and sober does not mean becoming perfect.

Nonetheless, it is important to acknowledge the fact that we are only human, and all we can do is the best that we can do, so that at the end of life's journey, we can say that we gave it our best shot, knowing our limitations, strengths and weaknesses, and we were the best human being that we could have been".

Change is hard for just about everyone, and some of our shortcomings will be painful to let go of. Trust me, I know I have one. Nonetheless, God will help you get through it (in his timing). In the meantime by you partnering with him, knowing that his grace is enough. Think back to all the painful things that you have overcome. The grace of God was there doing those times, and he is here now! Our higher power can restore us and make us whole. Remember when we came to believe this? It is important to let go of some of the stuff that weighs you down and stops you from enjoying your life. Consequently, when you were getting high or drinking, you really weren't living life therefore you very much needed to let that life style go.

Next, I want you all to be aware of the fact that sometimes the direction or the way that God wants to direct your life, may not be how or what you want. Nonetheless, know that it's all good, and he is doing what he knows is best for you. Find and treasure inner-peace and be still--child of God!

Boastfully speaking, this does not include what your spouse, kids, or friends think is best for you. This is God's will for your life. Our God knows when we are ready to move to a different level in life. Do we have to change? YES, because we cannot take that old abusive mentality into our future--flat out, it does not belong! You can not put new wine in old wine skin--what will happen--you answer that!

Humbleness will take you along the way on this road of recovery and what we called life. Allowing God to transform your life, will be one of the greatest experiences you'll ever have the pleasure of encountering and experiencing. Furthermore, while you are going through these changes, do not let ANYBODY tell you that God doesn't love or care about you. You child of God—are just as loved and wanted by him despite your shortcomings, as anybody else.

One last thing, since you have given up your will and partnered with God, confessed, have asked him to help you, and now humbling yourself, you will begin to notice your pride decreasing, because you will no longer misuse the gift of life. You may even fall in love, or are in love, but you will begin to love God more. People may make you upset, but you'll learn to turn the other cheek. You will begin to realize that you don't have to be jealous of anybody because your higher power has things for you too. Material things will no longer matter to you because you will grow to appreciate where they came from in the first place. I believe that these are some of the things that drove us to use. Being selfish, angry, jealous, childish, impatient, holding grudges, resentments, bitterness, abusive, victimizing, greedy, or having the spirit of entitlement, or lust. These are shortcomings, but nonetheless, we are overcomers. Humble yourself.

SOMETHING TO THINK ABOUT!

"You are an exceptional child of God. Therefore you will have exceptional problems, battles, trials, and tribulations. Everybody has contradictions, and EVERYBODY is a hypocrite about something"

Netheldia S Porter

Chapter 8

Fix Broken Relationships

Family, at some point or another we all must apologize for the things that we have done wrong to other people, especially if we are able to do so without causing more harm. This is how we restore broken relationships in our lives. Some will say "it is the beginning of the end". Nevertheless, apologizing allow us to be reintroduced to society, as well as into our families lives. Here my friends is where we start releasing the blame because we as addicts and alcoholics really believe that we are victims, and the problems in our lives are the direct result of somebody else. Let me state that I understand that many of us where traumatized and/or have childhood issues. However there is something I want you to remember "a lot of your childhood issues were inflicted by individuals who may have had childhood issues themselves". At any rate I hope that when you are ready, you will openly discuss those issues with your counselor, sponsor, or someone trustworthy, as well as God.

However right now I am referring to the harm that YOU caused another human being. Now are they a direct result of your childhood issues? Once again, this is something that can only be determined by you, and the person that you open these issues up to. Nonetheless as an adult, at one point or another, we have to be responsible for our own actions.

Throughout my life, I have discovered that we as addicts are very manipulative and we are good at creating scapegoats (someone to place the blame on). The greatest scapegoats is Jesus Christ he along took the blame for our wrong and went to the cross. However with us, everything is always someone else's fault and they are the reason we got high or drink. Sadly, due to this destructive, negative, false, made-up sense of reality and belief we have conjured up, we have HURT a lot of people, with this illusionary way we view life, people, places, things, and situations. As you may recall we already came to the realization that (we were powerless) over people, places and things. In addition, we as addicts and alcoholics created this false world in which we expect everybody else around us to survive in. In this world, we are the president, judge, jury, and the crucifixion.

Sadly while we were crucifying our loved ones or somebody else love ones, we cause major damage. Let me state that I am not here to get into the politics of the things you did that caused harm to another person and judge you, or put you down. I am about love! Therefore, now since we all understand each other, and without prejudice, I want to tell you that it is time to evacuate from Planet Sheree, Mark, Larry, Lisa or whatever your name may be, and come back or allow yourself to be introduced to PLANET EARTH, "the real world" --reality, and stop blaming because it's time to face-up to the harm you caused and apologize, (if it does not cause more harm to the individual or someone else).

Now some individuals that we have harmed have passed away. If this is your case, just simply tell God or someone you trust and ask him to forgive you. Some of us may want to just talk to the person at a grave site or wherever you may be, this is fine, but let me tell you that I believe "once a person goes into glory, all the bad things that happened to them while among the living, is not a part of where they have passed on to". I believe that they have already forgiven you.

Therefore you are just acknowledging the wrong and stating that you are sorry—freeing your conscious and forgiving ourselves--remember the freedom and good feeling about speaking stuff out loud so you can hear it. Let me point out that doing this type of amending is a personal decision that you will have to make for yourself because not everybody is comfortable with this. WARNING: If you knowingly have strong emotional feeling, guilt, shame, or regrets--PLEASE invite your counselor, sponsor, or someone else that you feel is a strong support in your life to be with while you are apologizing because sometimes when dealing with issues that concern people who have passed on, it may bring to life some painful memories or incidents.

Another thing, please do not beat yourselves up because we all make mistakes. You know, sometimes the hardest things for some of us to do, is forgiving ourselves. Remember this "God forgave us the first time we ask, therefore we are free to forgive ourselves-this is important.

Nonetheless, we cannot effectively move into our future, until we look at our past, and set things right. Once we do this, we can move into our future with peace of mind and freedom. By fixing broken relationships, we are able to let go of painful memories and things that haunt us, as well as the things that we "purposefully forget". You know that stuff that we push to the back of our minds because we don't want to think about them, or acknowledge the wrong we did or the role we played.

Remember earlier we were ready to confess, now it's time to come face to face with the individuals that we harmed (as long as it doesn't create more problems). Now truthfully, everybody may not be as forgiving as we may like. Therefore, don't get mad if your apology is not accepted. "At least you got it off of you, setting your own soul and spirit free".

Remember it's the individual's choice--which is between them and God. Which brings me to this point. In some situations you must be prepared to give an individual time. Will they forgive you in time? I do not know! You see we as addicts and alcoholics often times think just because we are fixed that everything should be alright immediately with everyone around us. NEWS FLASH! It doesn't work like that. We did a lot of damage, and carved some very painful scares in some people--some of them knee deep. These are the ones that only God and time can heal. So give people time to adjust to the new you, and the fact that you are living back here on planet earth!

For some individuals, you are going to have to be in reality for more than 30, 60, 90 or 180 days. For some it is going to take more than a year or two for them to not only forgive you, but trust you again as well AND THAT'S OKAY. Keeping it real, "there is not a scare like scars caused by a rage driven, ungrateful, untrustworthy, selfish addict or alcoholic, this is because most of these people are not just scared physically, but they are scared mentally and emotionally as well.

Some stuff we did even broke a person's spirit!

Can you recall what it felt like to be in love with someone or your first love? Well you remember how you felt when that relationship was over, or when you got your heart broken, or if they cheated on you. You know something like that! Well that's the same pain (if not worse) that we inflicted on people when we caused them harm or WORSE PAIN. Mind you, this is true whether they were related to you or not. Know this! Even people who you are not related can feel this kind of pain. Not only do you hurt them, but you also hurt their families and loved ones as well.

Think about it from this case scenario. The things that you did to people who were not your family members or may have been, would you want someone doing those things or worse to your dad, mom, sister, brother, son, daughter, grandchild, grandparents or spouse. Do you get the picture? How would that make you feel? This is the pain that some of us have inflicted on other people. So when you are making that list "BE FOR REAL".

Now I am not asking anyone to incriminate themselves, but you can talk to God, and set the record straight with him. Bottom line, making amends is part of moving on with your life. When you are actively working your program you would really want to leave all that negative stuff behind you.

We first must be willing to acknowledge our past, to know where we are going. try making a list, and then face every individual on that list. Please don't forget to closely examine the situations to make sure that asking for forgiveness will not cause harm to

the individual or another person.
 Lastly, don't beat yourself up about
the harm that you may have caused
another human being because many
people, even people who do not
abuse alcohol or drugs, forget or do
not live by the golden rules of
life:--"treat people how you want to
be treated" "if it doesn't belong to
you-don't touch it" "no means no",
and "have integrity". Remember
God's mercy is greater than anything
you have ever done wrong.

Something to think about!

"Victims are something that we want to
forget about. We want to drown out
everything that is painful and
unpleasant. There are two sides that face
off. First, we have the victims who wish
to forget but cannot. Then there's the
perpetrator who wants to escape
accountability for his or her crime, and
does everything in theirs power to
promote forgetting. Nonetheless it is
very painful for both. It has been found
that silence is the perpetrator's first line
of defense. If this fails, he or she then
attacks the credibility of their victim,
and gives an impressive array of
arguments, from the most stubbornness
of denial, to the most sophisticated and
cleverest of rationalization. Nonetheless,
after each crime, betrayal, assault etc, we
once again hear the expected and
predictable: it never happened, the
victim is lying, the victim is

exaggerating, or the victim brought it upon his or herself; and in any case the perpetrator strongly believes that it is time to purposefully forget and move on".

Netheldia S. Porter

Chapter 9

Take Care of The New You

Now truthfully soul searching, taking inventory, and apologizing should became a part of our everyday lives. It shows growth! So keep on top of you. It is a good thing for us to self-examine ourselves every once in a while. It is an important part of our sobriety because we are human, and we have and will make mistakes. By taking a personal inventory every once in a while, it enables us to continue to correct our wrong, and make amends more quickly and effectively then what we did during our addiction and alcohol abuse. Therefore we no longer have to be burdened down with guilt, shame or regret. We are now free to live our lives to the fullest DAILY.

Furthermore at this point we can effectively update our strengths and recognize new limitation as well as changes in our health because we do grow older physically and mentally. It is a good thing to know these things so we will not get caught up in situations we do not (A) want to be or (B) do not belong. We no longer have to stretch ourselves beyond our limits. Remember these things causes anger, frustration, bitterness, and resentment, and these things leads to RELAPSE. Importantly, know your triggers so you can deal with them at the onset.

Staying on top of ourselves allows us to improve the quality of our life on a continuous bases. It is a wonderful feeling being the best you!! It does not have anything to do with pride, but it has a lot to do with being alive, in reality here on

planet earth. Remember you are
your own worst enemy.

Something to think about!

"We grow from glory to glory" Don't trigger 10 steps backward

Netheldia S Porter

Chapter 10

Stay Connected To Him

The next principle I want to share with you, I take to heart because I believe it is one of the ways that we can maintain our sobriety. It is important to maintain a personal relationship with God. Furthermore, as this relationship grows, his will and plan for our lives will become clearer. In addition, as this plan becomes more visual to us, we will be equipped with everything we need to carry it out, and just for the record--we always had it in us, but we were so hypnotized by the power and influences of alcohol and drug abuse that we could not hear from God to carry out the plan that he had for our lives. Thank God for second chances!

What we need to do is keep praying and meditating to God, and make him apart of our daily lives from sunup to sundown, and taking every decision we make to him first. So daily drop to your knees and pray. Remember the glory is on the floor! I am not talking about religion or becoming a saint. No! I am talking about being spiritually connected to God, your higher power, just like you are connected to your family, lover, and friend because he is all of that and more.

There is something that I want you all to remember because I do not want you to get caught in a situation where you feel like you are not living up to other people's expectations rules or believes. This will cause you to feel worthless and hopeless, "which none of us are".

This is it, once you establish a connection with God, your higher power, do not allow outside influences to distract you from what you know God's will is for your life. When you know that you know that you know what God's plans and will is for your life--your purpose for living, just do what he says. I do not care how foolish, uncommon, not thought of, or impossible it may look to another individual or even yourself.

You do what God told you to do. If he can talk through the mouth of a donkey, trust me, you are of great value to him! Think about it like this, "he did not bring you through all the stuff he did, to get you to this point and be done with you". You may not be accepted by a lot of people because of your past, the stuff you did, or even because of who you are. He accepts you! Remember the connection that he have with him, is like no other. This is why I said "AS YOU UNDERSTAND HIM". If you have children, do you notice that they all are different — from the black sheep to the favored child? They all have different personalities, strengths, weakness, and limitations, and you just about know them all, right? Well, this is how our relationship is with God because no two people are alike, and he doesn't love one more than the other. Just as our children, they all have some sort of shortcoming or downfall but they belong to you right? You want the best for their life right? Well your God wants the best for your life.

He knows what you need, how you need it, and when you need it. Remember his will be done! He knows the right thing to do for you individually to carry out his will for your life and to live a fully victorious life--he knows what you don't.

My friend, it is also important to keep praying and spending time with God because he will give you directions day by day. The days when it seems like he is not talking or answering you, that means he may be testing you--so keep dotting the I's and crossing the T's--or do nothing--just wait. Nevertheless, during these times remember all that he has already told you and if he brought you out once, he'll do it again. Sit still and wait on your God, and just keep praying to him or do like I do sing to him during those dark, lonely, unsure, trying and testing times. Above all, always keep a relationship with God. Personally, I tried everything else, and I found that all I ever needed was him.

Something to think about!

Always give thanks to God who judges a man's heart, and allows his grace to be sufficient. He will not put more on us then we can bare.

Netheldia S. Porter

Chapter 11

Pass It On

Now you realized your powerlessness, the fact that you needed him and his will for your life. You came to realize you have shortcomings you needed to address, did some confessing, decided to work with God (and not against him) asked him to remove those shortcomings, made a list of people who you did wrong and apologize to them, realized that you have to always take care of yourself physically, mentally, emotionally, and spiritually, and that you must always and forever keep in contact with your higher power. **Congratulation!**

Now that you have allowed God to deliver, bless your life, and give you victory over the war against alcohol and drugs. GIVE IT BACK. When I say this I mean freely giving what has been so freely given to you. As you were helped, help somebody else who suffers from the disease of alcohol and/or drug abuse. The more you share, the more you keep it. To tell you the truth, when we finally realize the truth about addiction, it may bother us to see someone else suffering. We as recovering individuals will develop a natural desire to want to let people now who are still suffering. We want the world to know that there is a better way to live life and living abusive free is possible.

People every day live by these principles, recovering individuals and people who have never used in their life because these principles are reality, and they will help you live a peaceful prosperous, and effective life.

Something to think about!

It gets hard sometimes dealing with trials, tribulations, tests, and disappointments. However, the next time you feel pressured, overwhelmed, hopeless and wanting to quit. Do like a woman who is in labor does right before birth because after all you are working on birthing a new you-- when that next painful moment comes-- PUSH !!!

Netheldia S. Porter

ABOUT THE AUTHOR

Greetings, my name is Netheldia Sheree Porter. I was born on April 30 1965 and I am the oldest of 10 children. I have 3 daughters, two steps-sons and 7 grandchildren. I am happily married to my wife of 18 years. I grew up in Los Angeles California and spent most of my young adult life in Long Beach California. I dropped out of high school, but I have two college degrees one in Human Social Services and the other in Alcohol and Drug Studies. I have worked as a social worker for the County Of San Bernardino.

Sadly, I was molested as a child beginning at the age of 4 by neighborhood old men and late teenage women–no one ever knew.

I began abusing alcohol and drug when I was 9 years old, a lifestyle that took me down many avenues in which I would not wish on my worst enemy. Even though I came from a middle class family never wanting for nothing, I lived on skid row because of my addiction for a while and was in and out of several treatment centers. During the time that I was bound and incarcerated by these poisonous chemicals, I had three near death experiences, and was put in jail and prison more times than I care to remember.

Giving all praises to God, I have been off drugs for 25 years now. You see when I found out I was pregnant with my third child, I checked myself into my fourth treatment center because I refused to allow another child of mine to get caught up in the Child Protective Services

-and I had finally gotten tired of being a drug addict!

Speaking of children, my oldest daughter who is 35 now was in the child protective system a great deal of her life. Now she is a proud mother of 2, married, and works for that system herself as a supervisor. My 29 years old daughter who my sister took care of "off and on" is a proud mother of one, and is working on a Bachelor degree in business. My 25 year old daughter "whom I took care of from birth" is a proud mother of 3 and is working on her Bachelor degree in teaching. She is also married and lives with her husband on the Air Force base in Japan. My 24 year old step-son serves in the United States Army My 19 year old baby boy is a father and a Security Guard.

As you can tell I am very proud of my children, they went through a lot. Gracefully, we all have an outstanding relationship. A woman with my past could not have asked for a greater gift, than to be at peace with the children that she selfishly neglected, while abusing alcohol and drugs.

These girls look up to me, and admire me. God does answer prayers of restoration! I know that God has a special plan for my life.

I wrote "Something To Think About" because I wanted to reach people who struggle with addictions and all the problem that comes with it. I am living proof that a person can recover and live a fruitful life. If God helped me he'll help anybody.

God Bless, Keep and Favor you. This book is designed to speak to people who suffers from life, in a language that they can understand. No big words to figure out, just straight to the point. To add I have found that the skills in this book are practiced by people every day, therefore anybody who is struggling with anything can benefit from it. Remember–if you fall get back up because life happens!

SOMETHING TO THINK ABOUT!

"Our deepest fear is not that we are inadequate. Our deepest fear is that we are powerful beyond measure. It is our light, not our darkness that most frightens us. We ask ourselves, who am I to be brilliant, gorgeous, talented, and fabulous? Actually, who are you not to be? You are a child of God. We were born to manifest the glory of God within us. It is not just in some of us. It is in everyone. And as we let our own light shine, we unconsciously give other people permission to do the same. As we are liberated from our fear, our presence automatically liberates others"

Contact The Author

porterrialto@aol.com

OTHER CREATION

"Exceptional Child"- Winning Life's Journey. It is as raw as it gets **(not for kids) .**

Coming in 2021 -2022

"Total Victory"-at the end of it all"

Personal Prayers:

Personal Prayer:

Personal Prayers:

Personal Thoughts/Journal:

Personal Thoughts/Journal:

Inventory:

Inventory:

I apologizes:

I apologizes:

Important dates and meeting:

Short Team Goals:

Long Team Goals:

www.ingramcontent.com/pod-product-compliance
Lightning Source LLC
Chambersburg PA
CBHW032144040426
42449CB00005B/397